LEADER'S GUIDE

STUCK IN A RUT

POWER, SEX, FOOD AND OTHER LITTLE ADDICTIONS

WWW.ZONDERVAN.COM

Stuck in a Rut Leader's Guide: Power, Sex, Food and Other Little Addictions
Copyright © 2004 by Youth Specialties

Youth Specialties Books, 300 South Pierce Street, El Cajon, CA 92020, are published by
Zondervan, 5300 Patterson Aveune SE, Grand Rapids, MI 49530

Library of Congress Cataloging-in-Publication Data

Bundschuh, Rick, 1951-
  Stuck in a rut leader's guide : power, sex, food, and other little
addictions / by Rick Bundschuh.
      p. cm. -- (Highway visual curriculum)
    ISBN 0-310-25443-4 (pbk.)
  1. Church work with youth--Handbooks, manuals, etc. 2. Christian
education of young people--Handbooks, manuals, etc. 3. Audio-visual
education--Handbooks, manuals, etc. I. Title. II. Series.
  BV4447.B777 2004
  268'.433--dc22

                                                                          2003016310

Editorial and art direction by Rick Marschall
Edited by Laura Gross
Printed in the United States of America

03 04 05 06 07 08 09 / DC / 10 9 8 7 6 5 4 3 2 1

HIGHWAY VISUAL CURRICULUM

Volume Two

STUCK IN A RUT

Introduction

Welcome to Youth Specialties and Highway Video.

Unlike many teaching tools, Highway Video does not pre-sume to tell you what message to communicate to your flock. Instead, it is designed to be a flexible tool you can use to work with whatever message, purpose, and age level you have. Everything from announcements and teaching moments to benedictions, this material can be used with every age level—from middle school kids on up—and for just about any group size and church style.

But we don't want to leave you hanging.

In this booklet we've provided ideas for a variety of possible ways you can use each film clip. We've also included a lesson plan or two for you to check out and plug in wherever you feel it's appropriate. The lessons written for middle school students are short and action-filled. Those written for high school groups are longer with less action but more abstract thinking.

Our lesson plans even have downloadable, reproducible talk-sheets and other activity resources. You can download them for free off this Web site:
www.YouthSpecialties.com/store/downloads
code word: highway 2

To indicate each possible option for using a particular film clip, we've created a Signpost icon. This symbol designates a new path of teaching or communication for the video segment. With just a glance you'll be able to access a wide expanse of alternatives for using each video clip with your group.

Please feel free to manipulate the video in whatever way works best for your purposes.

For example, you may only want to show a portion of the video. Or you may decide that your group should view the clip more than once, maybe showing it to them a second time after you've explored the subject—just as a reminder.

You may download the video into your computer video editing program and clip the time, add a trailer, insert some Scripture, or use whatever device you have at your disposal that will help you communicate the point of your lesson or message.

Look for **Production Notes** and its icon to get behind-the-scenes comments from the producers.

For a couple of the Signposts we have gone ahead and mapped out lesson plans for youth groups that support a particular teaching idea inspired from the film clip. Remember, the talksheet resources for these lessons are integrated in these texts, but they can be downloaded and customized for your use free of charge at **www.YouthSpecialties.com/store/downloads code word: highway 2**

Today 1

Alternate Routes

 Emergent Ministries

Show the *Today* clip, which illustrates the need to slow down our lives and take time to listen to God on a regular basis. Then, to balance what the audience has just seen and as a lead-in to a time of silence and stillness before God, show the antithesis of the *Today* video—maybe you have a music video, MTV clip, or typical TV commercial.

▶ *Today* **Film Clip**

Small Group

Focus: Slowing down and being still before God.

Biblical basis: Psalm 4:4; Psalm 46:10; Psalm 119:97, 148

Stuff you need: Today video, discussion questions, Bibles

Getting Started

Ask your students to join you for a bit of silence. No talking, no noisemaking, no goofing around. (Don't tell your group how long the silence will go on for.) For some, one minute of silence will be a torture! After a minute or two or three (depending on your group) break the silence and ask—

> How long do you think we were silent for?

> How does silence make you feel?

> Why do you think many people are uncomfortable with their own thoughts during a time of silence?

> What does your mind do during a long silence?

Show the *Today* clip. Afterward, ask questions such as—

> What did you relate to in this video?

> What message do you think the creators of this piece were trying to communicate?

> Do you ever feel your life is way too busy for you to focus on the things that matter?

> Suggest some ways we can slow down or change our expectations so we don't live such harried lives.

Transition to the Bible study by saying something like this:

> **Let's take a look at a few powerful but simple ideas from Scripture about how to slow our lives down.**

Bible Study

Ask your group to read Psalm 4:4; Psalm 46:10; and Psalm 119:97, 148. Discuss the possible impact these passages could have on our daily schedules. Ask discussion questions such as—

When the writer of the Psalms asks us to be still, what would that mean to the life of a typical busy person?
What are the sounds you awaken to?

What things fill the stillness in your life?

How difficult would it be for you to drive to work or anywhere else in complete silence—without even the radio playing—while you considered who God is and what he wants for your life?

Describe how it's possible to be so busy doing God stuff that we leave out God.

Why do you think it's good to be still and silent before God?

Wrap Up

Ask your group to join you in a time of silence and meditation. Now that the group has read from the Psalms, maybe they have a thought on which to focus. But to reinforce the point of stillness, remind everyone that this might be an uncomfortable or awkward exercise for those people who have to fill their lives with sounds and activity, but there is a good chance God might speak to them in the silence.

Middle School

Focus: God wants us to take time to listen to him.

Biblical basis: Luke 10:38-42

Stuff you need: a box of stuff, *Today* video, Bibles, various art supplies, paper, 3x5 cards, pencils

Getting Started

How Much Can You Handle?

Get a box full of stuff that kids can pass to each other: balls, stuffed animals, tennis rackets, markers, books, and so on. Have your group sit in a circle and start by handing one of the kids several of the items to hold. The game begins as each kid passes the armful of stuff clockwise to the next kid. Each time the gear comes back around the circle to that first student, add several more items to the pile. Whenever a kid drops an item, he is out of the game. When someone is eliminated, the remaining kids should scoot closer together to tighten up the circle and then continue passing around all of the junk. The game doesn't end until you're left with one player who can juggle the most stuff.

Transition to the *Today* film clip by saying something like this:

> **Many adults—and kids—live lives that are very much like the game we just played, where they try to carry too many things during the course of a day. When your day-to-day existence is too full and busy, you don't have time to really enjoy life the way God intended or to concentrate on the important areas of life. Let's take a look at a short film that makes this point really well!**

Show the *Today* film clip. Afterward, ask a couple

Today		
vol	chp	pg
02:	01:	11

of questions such as—

> What was the problem for this girl?

> Can people be so busy doing good things that they're unable to do the best things? How?

Bible Study

Divide your students into groups of three to four and ask them to read the account of Mary and Martha from Luke 10:38-42. Each group should then work together to create a piece of art: a cartoon strip, a collage, a mural, a stained glass window made out of paper, or any other artistic creation you or your students can come up with that will effectively show what is taking place in this passage.

Pass out the necessary materials and let your students work for 10-15 minutes; then ask them to share the results.

After they have shared, ask—

> What was the problem with what Martha did?

> Why was what Mary did better than what Martha did?

> How can you and I do what Mary did?

Wrap Up

Pass out seven 3x5 cards and a pencil to each student. Ask the kids to go through the Bible and find seven verses—from either the New or the Old Testament—that seem kind of interesting or profound to them. They should write one verse on each index card.

Ask your kids to take the cards home; each morning or evening they should turn off their radio, TV, CD player, and any other noisemakers, and spend five minutes thinking about one of those verses and talking to God. In other words, they should commit to spend some time each day being a "Mary" person instead of a busy "Martha" person. Close in prayer.

 ## High School

Focus: Slowing down our busy lives in order to listen to God.

Biblical basis: Luke 10:38-42; Psalm 46:10

Stuff you need: *Today* video, Today Talksheets, pencils, Bibles, paper *(Note: You can download the talksheet from* www.YouthSpecialties.com/store/downloads *code word:* highway 2 *and photocopy it to use with your group.)*

Getting Started

Idea #1: Ask your kids to find a partner. Give them some time to describe to each other their audio and visual environment on a typical day. Do they wake up to music? Is the TV always on at their houses? Do they listen to music on the way to school or at work? Do they watch lots of TV, listen to music, or spend time on a computer when they're at home? Do they fall asleep to music? Ask a few of your students to share what they learned about their partner's daily routine.

Transition to the *Today* film clip by saying something like this:

> **It is very common in our modern culture to surround ourselves with noise and activity all day long. When we add this type of audio stimula-**

Today

vol chp pg
02: 01: 13

tion to our already busy schedules, we often find that our days become loaded with duties but void of depth. Let's take a look at a film that does a great job of bringing out this idea.

Show the *Today* film clip.

Idea #2: Ask your students to take a look at the "Outa Time" talksheet. Ask them to circle any of the statements that are true in their lives. Or just read the statements aloud and have your students respond by raising their hands if they agree with them.

Outa Time

Circle any of the following statements that are true in your life:

I carry a full schedule at school.

I work a job after school or on weekends.

I have chores that I am expected to do around the house.

I spend at least an hour each night on homework.

I attend midweek youth activities at my church.

I am involved in extra curricular school activities that take place after school.

I am on a sports team.

I am involved in projects or groups that keep me busy at least one night a week.

I have little free time to just goof around.

I have a steady boyfriend/girlfriend.

I participate in other activities at my church besides the youth group.

Ask your students—

> If your life seems really busy and full, is this a
> good thing or a bad thing?

> When does it become too much?

Transition to the *Today* film clip by saying something like this:

> **Let's take a look at a life full of good things that
> still seems to be spinning out of control. Show
> the *Today* film clip.**

Bible Study

Idea #1: Split your group in half and ask them to
read the account of Mary and Martha from Luke
10:38-42. Hand out paper and pencils to each student. Assign one group of students to create—
individually—what might have been Mary's diary
entry for that particular day with Jesus; the other
group should create Martha's diary entry from that
day.

Ask students to share any insights they may have
come up with while looking at the Scripture in this
fashion. Now discuss some of these ideas:

> What was the core message Jesus gave to
> Martha?

> What do you think God wants to say to people
> who are busy doing good things?

> How do we become more like Mary?

Today

vol   chp   pg
02: 01: 15

What does it mean to "sit at the feet of Jesus"?

What changes might a person make to be like Mary in this regard?

Idea #2: Challenge your students to abandon the busyness of their young lives by going on an instant meditative retreat. Warn them that if they're used to having noise and images fill their days, this may be an uncomfortable experience for them. Before launching into the idea, share Psalm 46:10 with your group: "Be still, and know that I am God; I will be exalted among the nations, I will be exalted in the earth."

Find an area where your students can spread out so they won't be distracted by one another. An outdoor location is best but not essential. You may even want to leave your church campus in order to find the right quiet spot. Make sure each person has brought a Bible and chosen a portion of Scripture to mull over during the retreat time.

Before the group spreads out, go over the ground rules with them:

Silence is to be observed.

The time should be spent praying silently, thinking about their passage of Scripture, or listening for what God might be whispering to them.

Allow enough time for the group to come back together and talk about what they experienced.

Wrap Up

Invite your students to read and sign "The Challenge of Silence" found on the talksheet (see below). By signing it, they'll pledge to spend a week without music or television in order to make their hearts available to hear God.

The Challenge of Silence

I _____ willingly accept the challenge to go for the next week without intentionally listening to music or watching television, videos, and DVDs. I am doing this in order to allow my mind and heart a chance to hear God's quiet voice speak to me in spite of a busy life.

Plan to follow up next week and give them time to talk about how they responded to the challenge. Close in prayer.

Idea #2: Ask your students to quietly take an inventory of their lives. Urge those kids whose lives resemble the girl on the *Today* video to commit to lightening their load by dropping at least one activity in order to better enjoy their relationship with God and what he has planned for their lives. Close in prayer.

Production Notes

Producer Kevin Marks

Out here in California, everyone is busy. Even two-year olds have Palm Pilots and personal administrative assistants, and high school students live with cell phones attached to their faces. Well, almost. Juggling responsibilities with school, academics, sports, youth groups, clubs, and homework can not only drive you crazy, but can deteriorate your health and damage your relationships.

So where does God fit in? Do we have time to explore and experience God in a world so amok with the business of life? Did God design us to be pushed to the limit? We don't think so, yet it's a problem that we're faced with through adulthood and beyond. The cool thing is, though, that high school students can take control of their schedules and set positive patterns for their lives that will continue until they're old and gray, watching Wheel of Fortune reruns in their RV.

We sent Ryan Pettey out to capture what life is like for the average overworked high school student. We hope it serves as a wake-up call--to remind you to give some time over to God. As busy as you are in high school, it only gets busier, so take time to be young, and to be young with God.

Food Fight 2

Alternate Routes

General Church Use –

Food Fight is a perfect starter clip to use in home Bible study settings or Sunday school for just about any age group. Make sure workers from children's ministries to adult ministries have a chance to see this resource.

Emergent Ministries

Do you need a bit of humor to illustrate how we can see everyone's problems but our own? While each situation may require different timing, this film clip is a great opening piece for a message and can be very effective without any set up at all. Subject matters that will work well with this clip: judgment, criticism, addiction, or gluttony.

Small Group

A small group setting will provide a great opportunity for meaty discussions about the message of this video. Here is an outline you can utilize to get a small group rolling.

Focus:	Solving our own problems before we start to criticize others.
Biblical basis:	Matthew 7:1-5
Stuff you need:	*Food Fight* video, Bibles, discussion questions

Getting Started

The *Food Fight* film clip is a great opener for a discussion-based Bible study. Get your group comfortable and let the show begin!

Follow up with discussion questions such as—

Underneath the humor of this film, there is an important message. What do you think it is?

What were they complaining about?

Why is it that we don't see our own hang-ups but we are quick to see the hang-ups of others?

Roll into the Bible study with this question:

Can you think of a humorous teaching of Jesus that makes the same point?

Bible Study

Read Matthew 7:1-5 and kick around what Jesus meant by "judging" as well as the idea that we need to take a hard look at our weak spots before playing the "I'm-better-than-you" game with others.

Use questions like the following examples to get the mental wheels turning:

A lot of non-Christians quote the first part of this passage from Matthew as a stab at Christians who take strong stands on issues such as homosexuality, abortion, adultery, and so on. Based on this verse, do you think Christians shouldn't set standards of right and wrong for anyone other than themselves? Why or why not?

Why do you think this a popular verse with unbelievers?

What picture does the whole context of this passage give us on what it means to "judge" a person?

What are we told we should do before trying to help someone who is struggling with his or her "speck"? Give a real life example of how this would work.

Wrap Up

Help your group figure out how to correct the blind spots many of us have about our own behavior. Ask—

How do you know if you have a log in your eye?

How does the Bible help us see ourselves for who we really are?

How should our Christian friends help us see ourselves for who we really are?

What's the hardest part about being honest about our own shortcomings?

Ask your group to select one of the following tactics and commit to try it this week as an exercise in avoiding that old log-eye trap.

1. Spend some time reading the Bible—not to gain more knowledge, but to hear what God is saying to you *about* you.

2. Pick a wise friend or mentor and give him or her permission to speak hard truth to you whenever he she thinks you need to hear it.

3. Take some time to think before you open your mouth to criticize someone.
Close in prayer.

Middle School

Focus: Taking a long and honest look at ourselves before we put down others.

Biblical basis: Matthew 7:1-5

Stuff you need: blindfolds, plastic spoons, jars of baby food, towels, garbage bags, Bibles, markers, 3x5 cards, paper and pencils

Getting Started

This opening game can be an object lesson for everyone or a contest between a few pairs of kids. Choose the students you want to participate and pair them up. Have them sit in chairs facing each other. Give one kid a jar of baby food and a plastic (easier on the teeth) spoon. Blindfold both kids. Except to hold the bottle and spoon, no hands can be used. (Caution: This can be a messy stunt. Prepare for lots of slop.) At your signal the kid holding the baby food is to feed his or her blind partner. The cleanest pair or the pair finished first wins.

Transition to the Bible study by saying something like this: Did you notice why this is so messy? When you can't see clearly, you tend to make a mess. With that thought in mind, let's watch a film clip that is also food related.

▶ *Food Fight* Film Clip

Tell your students that the *Food Fight* clip is a humorous *parable* that they should try to figure out.

Show the clip and see what kind of conclusions they draw from it.

Food Fight
vol chp pg
02: 02: 23

Ask questions such as—

> Underneath the humor of this film, there is an important message—what do you think it is?

> What were they complaining about?

> Why is it that we don't see our own hang-ups but we are quick to see the hang-ups of others?

 ## Bible Study

Divide everyone into smaller groups of three to four students and pass out markers and paper to each. Ask the groups to read Matthew 7:1-5 and create a cartoon that illustrates the message Jesus was teaching. After a few minutes, have your groups share their comic creations.

Turn the concept toward everyday life by asking your groups to huddle together and come up with an example of how someone could be critical of others but not see their own mess-ups in the same area. Ask them to share their ideas.

Wrap Up

Pass out 3x5 cards and ask the students to write a short instruction or command to themselves called "The Log Eye Check." This card should be a summation, based on what they've learned from the lesson, of what they need to do before they blast some other person with criticism or a thumbs-down judgment. Ask the students to take their cards home and post them where they will serve as a reminder of how to treat others.

High School

Focus: Taking a long and honest look at ourselves before we put down others.

Biblical basis: Matthew 7:1-5; Romans 2:1.

Stuff you need: a chalkboard or a large piece of paper and something to write with; Bibles, Food Talksheets; paper and pencils
(Note: You can download the Talksheet from www.YouthSpecialties.com/store/downloads *code word: highway 2 and photocopy it to use with your group.)*

Getting Started

Idea #1: Ask your group to suggest some words non-Christians use to describe their idea of Christians. Write them down on a large piece of paper or chalkboard so everyone can see them. You may get a number of suggestions—both good and bad—but most likely the word "judgmental" will appear somewhere in the mix. Take a few minutes to discuss which of these ideas held about Christians are based in reality and which are misconceptions.

Transition to the *Food Fight* film clip by saying something like this:

> **A lot of people have critical views of others while they never see their own problems. Let's take a look at a film clip that is a humorous parable about that very subject.**

Idea #2: Start by showing the *Food Fight* film clip, but before you do, divide your students into a "listening group" and a "looking group." The listening group should pay attention to what is said and record the number of different subjects that are discussed by the guys in the car. The looking group should count the number of different items

Food Fight

vol   chp   pg
02: 02: 25

of food that are shown in the film.

After the clip is finished, ask—

How many different food items were in this video?

What subjects were being discussed?

What do you think this goofball parable was about?

 Bible Study

Idea #1: Beforehand, cut strips from the "Who's to Judge?" talksheet (or just copy the statements onto 3x5 cards—you can always add more). Put the strips or cards into a container for later.

Pass out paper and pencils and ask the students to write a critical review of the film. (Share the production notes at the bottom of this lesson to give the kids more ammo for their critiques.) This activity will draw out the idea, which is so humorously depicted in the film clip and covered more seriously by the words of Jesus, of how we can be critical of others but blind to our own shortcomings. Read their reviews.

Tackle the subject of sitting in judgment from another angle by having your students get into groups of three to four. Ask your students to read Matthew 7:1-5 and Romans 2:1 on their own. Because many unbelievers (and even a few Christians) use this passage to improperly imply that Christians are violating their own standards if they weigh in on the actions or behaviors of others, it is important to spend a little time helping students figure out what thinking is sound. After your students have finished reading the passage ask them—

What do you think this passage is teaching?

Is it ever right to judge or be a critic? When and why?

Ask each group to select one of the "Who's to Judge?" question strips or cards and discuss within their group if it would be wrong to "judge" the actions or behavior of the person described on it.

Who's to be Judged?

A pregnant unmarried teenager

A kid who cheats on his history final and gets caught

A Christian kid who gets drunk at a party

A friend who steals something from you

A friend who is interested in the person you are dating

A kid who wastes all day playing video games

A person who drugs and rapes a girl at a party

A kid selling drugs

A kid who loses control and swears at another kid

A friend who tells one of your secrets

A sibling who ruins your favorite CD or sports gear or article of clothing

A kid who takes credit for something you did

A parent who abandons their family to have an affair

An uncle who molests your little sister

A friend who now thinks they are too good for your group

Probe their responses with questions such as—

> Are there some situations that call for mercy,
> understanding, and sympathy rather than hard-
> core judgment?

> What is the difference between a small act of evil
> and a large one? Should they be thought of any
> differently?

> What difference would it make in our culture if
> everyone lived by the secular idea of zero judging,
> complete tolerance, and everything goes, versus
> the biblically accurate idea of judging with the
> expectation and understanding that you will be
> judged by the same manner and criteria?

Idea #2: Ask your students to form groups of
three to four and read Matthew 7:1-5 and Romans
2:1. Distribute paper and pencils and ask each
small group to come up with a practical list of
instructions to be included in a pamphlet called,
"How Not to be a Log Eye." Give the groups time
to work and then ask them to share their efforts.

Discuss the ideas of this passage by asking questions such as—

> What do you think this passage is teaching?

> Is it ever right to judge or be a critic? When and
> why?

Wrap Up

Idea #1: Pass out copies of the "My Best
Response" talksheet and pencils. Invite your students to look over the statements and—without

discussion or the need to share—circle the statement that best reflects the desire and prayer of their hearts.

Close in prayer.

My Best Response

Please circle the statement that best represents the desire of your heart.

When it comes to being critical of others...

This is an area where I really need God's help to change my attitude.

I want to stop and think about what I say before I say it.

I want to be better able to discern the difference between the sinner and the sin.

I want to get my problems worked out before I start getting critical of the problems of others.

When it comes to my own weaknesses...

I want genuine friends who will level with me about the places where I'm not cutting it.

I want to have a real picture of who I am and what I am like, and I am willing for God to show me.

I need someone to whom I can be accountable and who will prevent me from being crushed by my own selfishness.

Idea #2: The characters in the *Food Fight* video obviously didn't know themselves very well. Give your students a chance to see if they can do any better. Hand out slips of paper or cards and ask them to fill in the blank for each statement you read.

I am most likely to go to excess in the area of

_____.

My thoughts can get the best of me when

_____.

The one thing I pray God will change about me is

_____.

Production Notes: Food

Producer/Director Ryan Pettey

The *Food Fight* video was shot in two days with over $60 worth of food. Ryan and Anthony ate so much food during the filming of this video that between each take they would usually spit out the food into a huge metal bowl (or out the window onto the beautiful streets of Santa Barbara). Though stuffing your face gluttonously may seem like a great way to spend a day, the constant three-point turns, near fender benders (due to Ryan's patented "Film and Drive" technique), and sucking on whipped cream cans proved too much for Ryan's and Anthony's stomachs. Towards the end of the second day they both wanted to puke—proving, once again, that gluttony never pays.

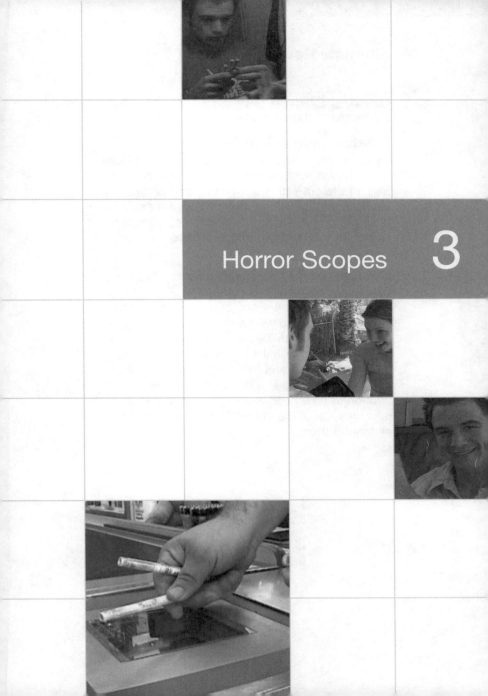

Horror Scopes 3

Alternate Routes

General Church Use and Emergent Ministries —

A Satire on New Age Thinking

Use the whole video or just grab the first minute or so of the *Horror Scopes* film clip (you'll have to add a fade out with your own editing gear). It's a satire on the foolish lengths people will go to in their search for wisdom or guidance, when the source of true wisdom and guidance is God's Word.

If you are heavy into visuals and your theme is God's guidance or getting to know God's will for your life, you may want to consider combining the *Horror Scopes* clip with a short, hilarious scene from *The Man With Two Brains*. In it, Steve Martin's character asks his dead wife's picture to give him a sign if she thinks it's okay if he starts dating. This scene is a great—and funny—demonstration of how people only hear what they *want* to hear, in spite of the contradictory evidence that's all around them.

Small Group

Focus: Who guides us?

Biblical basis: Exodus 15:13; Psalm 25:5,9; Psalm 31:3; Psalm 32:8; Isaiah 48:17

Stuff you need: *Horror Scopes* video, Bibles, pencils and paper

Getting Started

Explain to your group, that not everyone consults the Bible when looking for answers. Ask your group to name some dumb things people will try when they desperately want guidance for their lives. (You may hear—read horoscopes, read tea leaves, consult Ouija boards, read tarot cards, talk to a palm reader, talk to a guru, just follow their hearts, and so on.)

Introduce the *Horror Scopes* film clip by saying something like this: Here's a short send-up of a product most of you have seen. Probably no one you know takes it seriously—yet *somebody* keeps purchasing them!

▶ *Horror Scopes* Film Clip

After the film clip ends, ask—

What idea were the filmmakers lampooning?

Do you think people buy mini scrolls for guidance or to have a good laugh?

Why do you think many newspapers run horoscopes?

Use these questions to roll into a discussion about God's guidance and create a transition to the Bible study.

Bible Study

Ask your group to read the following passages of Scripture and come up with a one-sentence message that sums up what they think God wants to communicate to all human beings who are trying to navigate life without reliable guidance: Exodus 15:13; Psalm 25:5,9; Psalm 31:3; Psalm 32:8; and Isaiah 48:17. Give your group a chance to share their summations, then discuss why people (and sometimes believers) are so hesitant or unwilling to allow God to be their guide.

Ask questions such as—

Why do you think people run to all kinds of odd—even nutty—people and things for guidance in their lives while they ignore God?

Do you think most people really want guidance, or do they merely want confirmation of their own wills and desires?

What are the primary ways God guides us?

What is the scary thing about allowing God to guide us?

What is the comforting thing about allowing God to guide us?

How deep in the nitty-gritty things of life do you think God's guidance goes? Whom we should date or marry? What kind of car we drive? How we spend our money? The kind of toothpaste we buy?

Is God's guidance usually specific in nature, or does it merely contain general principles to live by? Which puts more demands on a human?

Wrap Up

Ask your students to think of one area in their lives

where they need guidance. This does not have to be a huge issue; it can be something simple or small. With that thought in mind, you may either ask the group to share their areas with others and ask for prayer, or they may simply hold the thought inside and seek God's specific guidance on that subject during the closing time of prayer.

Getting Started

The Guidance Game

 Middle School

Focus: Where to find genuine guidance in life.

Biblical basis: Psalm 23

Stuff you need: 3x5 cards, pencils, a big bowl or box, *Horror Scopes* video, paper, Talksheets, pre-cut colored paper strips, Bibles
(Note: You can download the talksheet from www.YouthSpecialties.com/store/downloads code word: highway 2 *and photocopy it to use with your group.)*

Pass out 3x5 cards to the students and ask them to write down an instruction for someone else in the group to carry out. (Note: if you have a small class you may want to invite kids to write a number of instruction cards.)

Rules for creating the instructions are—

The assignment must be able to be done within the room and with any props at hand.

It cannot be gross or obscene in nature.

The leader has the right to modify any instruction.

You MUST follow the instructions if your name is picked.

Horror Scopes

When they've finished, have the students fold the cards and put them into a container. You may also load the deck with instruction cards of your own creation to make things more fun.

Pick a kid at random, draw a card for him or her, then read the instruction out loud. (It's usually best for a leader to draw and read the cards in case they need to be edited or improvised.) The student must then do whatever the card says. After the instructions have been carried out satisfactorily, allow that kid to pick the next victim—er, student—until all have been selected.

After this goofy and embarrassing game ends, transition to the film clip by asking questions such as—

> Under what circumstances would you be willing to let a stranger guide your life? What if the stranger were a police officer, doctor, or firefighter?
>
> Do you think most kids make their own decisions, or are they more heavily influenced by friends, family, and media? Why or why not?
>
> Describe what a horoscope is. Who writes them, and why do people allow these strangers to guide the actions of their lives?
>
> What do believers in horoscopes do?
>
> You may want to show an actual mini scroll or newspaper horoscope to your students and read a bit of it to your kids as many of them may not be familiar with this kind of thing.

▶ *Horror Scopes* Film Clip

Invite your students to watch the satirical *Horror Scopes* film clip. Let them know in advance that the filmmakers are making fun of people who hold nutty ideas such as this one, while they also hope to prod people to ask the question, *Who guides my life decisions?*

After the film, transition to the Bible study by saying something like this: While this film shows how crazy it is to trust your future to a dumb horoscope, a lot of us hang around with friends who don't have much better guidance in their lives.

 ## Bible Study

Invite your class to take a short "Guidance Test" below, or downloadable from www.YouthSpecialties.com/store/downloads code word: highway 2 or copy and use the following sample.

Guidance Test

For each statement below, circle the number that most *honestly* represents your friends (#1 = almost never and #5 = all the time):

My friends usually do what the rest of the gang does.

1   2   3   4   5

When my friends need advice about something the first place they go is to their parents.

1   2   3   4   5

Most of my friends try to follow the Bible as their guide in life.

1   2   3   4   5

I think my friends are influenced to do, think, and say things by TV, movies, and other media.

1   2   3   4   5

I think my friends would say they don't need much help or guidance in life; they pretty much have things figured out.

1   2   3   4   5

Talk a little bit about the questions in the quiz and
see if you can get a feeling for how your students
rate their friends, which often matches how they
would rate themselves as well.

Break up into groups of four to five kids and ask
each group to read Psalm 23. Now hand out paper
and pencils to the groups and ask them to read
through the psalm again as they create a list of all
the good stuff that comes from letting God lead
us. Then—using that list of benefits—they should
create a full-page magazine ad that invites people
to stop heading down those dead-end paths (like
following stupid stuff like horoscopes) and give
God a try.

Wrap Up

Give each student a strip of colored paper that is
pre-cut to the approximate size and shape of a
mini scroll. Invite them to use the paper to create
an alternative to the mini scroll (whose wisdom is
indeed mini, if not altogether non-existent). Call it
the "Mega Scroll." The Mega Scroll ought to contain wisdom and advice taken from the Bible
about as many issues and ideas as they can come
up with. At the end, have kids roll up their Mega
Scrolls and take them home for future reference.
Close in prayer.

Getting Started

Idea #1: In advance, in a vacant room or hallway, form a grid or maze using twine stretched and zig-zagged across the space at a height that is just

High School

Focus: Where to find genuine guidance in life.

Biblical basis: Exodus 15:13; Psalm 23; Psalm 25:5,9; Psalm 31:3; Psalm 32:8-10; Isaiah 48:17

Stuff you need: twine or yarn, blindfolds, a prize, *Horror Scopes* video, talksheets, large sheet of paper, Bibles, paper and pencils

above the students' head level. Have a number of blindfolds on hand and a staff person or two who are ready to assist only the kids *who ask for help*. Make sure the twine (you could also use yarn) is tied securely to the wall so it can't be yanked out.

As students enter the room, blindfold them or ask them to close their eyes (if you think they can be trusted). Then place one of their fingers on the twine and tell them that the object of the maneuver is to get from the starting point (this location should vary with each student) to the exit door without hitting a dead end or taking their finger off the twine. Let them know a special prize is waiting for the person who makes the best time through the maze without cheating; then casually mention that there is a personal guide *available upon request.*

Have fun escorting kids through the hall or room and watching those who would rather do it without help—even though it means they could lose their shot at a prize. Make sure the guides know it is their job to get those students who request help to the exit in the quickest possible time.

Award the prize. Transition to the film clip by saying something like this: You no doubt are wondering what we're up to with that string maze. Well, this is just a way to get you thinking about life and the fact that without a guide, each of us is going through it blind. And funny enough, some people who are looking for guidance reach out to things that put them even more in the dark. We will see an example of this in a short, satirical film clip called *Horror Scopes*. Show the *Horror Scopes* film clip.

Idea #2: Make copies of the talksheets and pass them out to your students. Ask them to find their birthdates and read what the horoscope says about them. Or, before your group meets, take some lines from the Bad News Horoscope section at the end of the talksheet and cut and paste them into the genuine article (just for fun). Or you can also use only the dumb stuff to create a whole new horoscope to hand out.

Jump into a discussion about horoscopes with some questions such as—

What do you notice about the descriptions given?

What do you think of people who take these seriously?

Why do you think horoscopes are attractive?

What's Your Sign, Ba-by?

This is a genuine Horoscope. Find your Birthday and see what kind of kooky things it tries to pawn off as good guidance. Take special note of the phony sameness, the flattering buzz words, the New Age nonsense--and realize that this is all dangerous, not just foolish.

Aries March 21 - April 19

* Your Most Likeable traits: Courage, Natural Leader & an Exciting Doer

* SYMBOL: The Ram (Assertive, sexual, able to climb to great heights)

* Element: Fire

* Dominant Keyword: I AM.

* Magical Birthstone: Diamond (Attracts love, financial success,brings luck in new ventures. The diamond is particularly lucky for Aries people when worn on the left side of the body.)

* Special Flowers: Geranium, Honeysuckle & Sweet Pea

* Lucky Numbers: 1 & 9

* Lucky Day: Tuesday

Taurus April 20 - May 20

* Your Most Likeable traits: Dependable, Creative & Emotionally Sensitive

* SYMBOL: The Bull (Strong, stubborn, plodding, can be both fierce and gentle.)

* Element: Earth

* Dominant Keyword: I HAVE.

* Magical Birthstone: Emerald (Protects against infidelity & deceit, insures loyalty & improves memory.)

* Special Flowers: Violet, Poppy & Lily of the Valley

* Lucky Numbers: 6 & 4

* Lucky Day: Friday

Gemini May 21 - June 20

* Your Most Likeable trait: Responsiveness, Great Communicator & a True Humanitarian

* SYMBOL: The Twins (Associated with duality, humanism, versatility, communication)

* Element: Air

* Dominant Keyword: I THINK

* Magical Birthstone: Agate (A multicolored precious stone that protects from deception & falsehood & bestows eloquence, especially in declarations of love.)

* Special Flowers: Lily of the Valley, Rose & Lavender

* Lucky Numbers: 5 & 9

* Lucky Day: Wednesday

Cancer June 21 - July 22

* Your Most Likeable traits: Loyal, Sensitive & Family-oriented

* SYMBOL: The Crab (Possessing an impenetrable exterior covering soft flesh underneath)

* Element: Water

* Dominant Keyword: I FEEL.

* Magical Birthstone: Moonstone & Pearl (Changes bad fortune into good & discord into harmony. It also brings support from influential people.)

* Special Flowers: Larkspur & Acanthus

* Lucky Numbers: 3 & 7

* Lucky Day: Monday

Leo July 23 - Aug 22

* Your Most Likeable trait: Generosity, Exuberance, Born Entertainer

* SYMBOL: The Lion (Regal, brave, dominating,

sometimes insolent. Possessing nobility and pride.)

* Element: Fire

* Dominant Keyword: I WILL.

* Magical Birthstone: Ruby (Protects against physical injury & insures faithfulness. It also brings its wearer serenity of mind.)

* Special Flowers: Sunflower, Marigold & Gladiolus

* Lucky Numbers: 8 & 9

* Lucky Day: Sunday

Virgo Aug 23 - Sept 22

* Your Most Likeable traits: Conscientious, Organized & Energetic

* SYMBOL: The Virgin (Representing purity, modesty, industriousness, service to fellow workers.)

* Element: Earth

* Dominant Keyword: I ANALYZE.

* Magical Birthstone: Sapphire (Brings tranquility of mind & protects against illness & injury while traveling.)

* Special Flowers: Morning Glory & Pansy

* Lucky Numbers: 5 & 3

* Lucky Day: Wednesday

Libra Sept 23 - Oct 22

* Your Most Likeable traits: Charming, Diplomatic, Easy-going

* SYMBOL: The Scales (Balance, Equilibrium, Order, and Justice)

* Element: Air

* Dominant Keyword: I BALANCE.

* Magical Birthstone: Opal (Brings financial success, frees its wearer from jealousy & greed & imparts

clear insight.)

* Special Flowers: Rose, Cosmos & Hydrangeas

* Lucky Numbers: 6 & 9

* Lucky Day: Friday

Scorpio Oct 23 - Nov 21

* Your Most Likeable traits: Idealistic, Dedicated & Intense

* SYMBOL: The Scorpion (A secretive, deadly creature that can poison its enemies)

* Element: Water

* Dominant Keywords: I DESIRE.

* Magical Birthstone: Topaz (Releases occult powers & brings serenity of mind. It also protects from enemies & illness)

* Special Flowers: Chrysanthemum & Rhododendron

* Lucky Numbers: 2 & 4

* Lucky Day: Tuesday

Sagittarius Nov 22 - Dec 21

* Your Most Likeable traits: Optimistic, Independent & Adventurous

* SYMBOL: The Archer (Representing directness, high aims, a love of the heavens)

* Element: Fire

* Dominant Keyword: I SEE.

* Magical Birthstone: Turquoise (Attracts love, protects from harm & gives its wearer the ability to see into the future)

* Special Flowers: Narcissus, Holly & Dandelion

* Lucky Numbers: 5 & 7

Capricorn Dec 22 - Jan 19

* Your Most Likeable traits: Steadiness, Superb Organizer, Practical

* SYMBOL: The Goat (A surefooted animal who is able to ascend the heights by taking advantage of every foothold)

* Element: Earth

* Dominant Keyword: I USE.

* Magical Birthstone: Garnet (Attracts popularity, high esteem & true love)

* Special Flowers: Carnation & Ivy

* Lucky Numbers: 2 & 8

* Lucky Day: Saturday

Aquarius Jan 20 - Feb 18

* Your Most Likeable traits: Friendly, People-oriented, Outgoing

* SYMBOL: The Water bearer (Dispensing a gift that flows freely equally to all: Representing creation & the giving of life)

* Element: Air

* Dominant Keyword: I KNOW.

* Magical Birthstone: Amethyst (Brings faithfulness in love & bestows the gift of prescience)

* Special Flower: Orchid & Violet

* Lucky Numbers: 1 & 7

* Lucky Day: Wednesday

Pisces Feb 19 - Mar 20

* Your Most Likeable traits: Compassionate, Sensitive & Spiritual

* SYMBOL: Two Fishes (Tied to one another & swimming in opposite directions)

* Element: Water

* Dominant Keyword: I BELIEVE.

* Magical Birthstone: Aquamarine (Magnifies occult
powers & brings serenity of mind. Also protects its
wearer while traveling on the sea

* Special Flowers: Water Lily, White Poppy & Jonquil

* Lucky Numbers: 2 & 6

* Lucky Day: Friday

The Bad News Horoscope--It's just what you deserve!

Everyone will avoid you, even though your personality
isn't infectious.

The extreme monotony of your life will cause you to hal-
lucinate.

You have large reserves of smug self-satisfaction and
suppressed feelings of superiority. Draw on these
resources. Accept the fact that you will never fully
understand why others are so inferior to you.

Only use moderation in moderation.

In some ways, yesterday seems long ago;

In other ways it seems like only yesterday....

Optimists will pretend you're invisible.

You will develop a sense of humor and die laughing at
yourself.

Your long life will reflect the advantages of dying young.

You are the Chosen One, just like you always suspected.

Look to premature senility to save your self-respect.

Look to be pleasantly surprised sometime around mid-
May, 2023.

Close friends will surprise you tonight with the absence
of a party.

You're a horrible monster trapped in a human body.

Take comfort in the saying "beauty is only skin deep"

Tell yourself that a dull life is a sign of a fulfilled person.

A rare conjunction of stars means bad luck for the rest of your life.

A trusted friend will outlive you.

Your world is a miserable, doomed place.

Do whatever you want. You don't matter.

A disfiguring car accident will improve your looks.

You were born the wrong sex.

You will soon be able to do all the things sane people can do.

As a member of the world conspiracy, you control your own future.

Events later this year will prove your life isn't as bad as it could be.

All your fantasies will come true after your imagination is surgically removed.

The simple life is your key. It will make you miserable.

You're too unstable to understand yourself, much less calculus or other people.

You'll change your definitions of "fat" and "ugly" to save your self-respect.

Neurologists will discover that the voices you hear in your head are only echoes.

Your hopes and your future have nothing in common.

Your dog finds you repulsive.

You will meet your perfect mate today. Congratulations! It's yourself.

Very large doses of radiation could release power hidden in your dormant genes.

Sixty years from now, you'll start to doubt that the only way to fail in life is by not trying.

You'll never find out whether you're miserable because you're a failure or vice versa.

People who believe, "If you can't say anything nice, don't say anything at all," will refuse to talk to you.

Listen to your instincts, and do the opposite.

Over the next few decades you'll convince people to stop pretending that survival requires courage, intelligence and wisdom.

Your loved ones will donate your corpse to science while you're still healthy.

Cannibalism suits you.

You deserve to be disappointed.

Your fish resents your control over its life.

You will become obsessively self-conscious about those knobby knees.

You will be thrown out of the sanitarium when your family refuses to pay.

You have a knack for doublethink that you never realized you had. In fact, you will never realize it.

Your lucky number is 511. Play the lottery every day, because you have no talents, and unless dumb luck makes you rich, people will continue to shun you.

Your multiple personalities don't prevent you from being dull.

Never argue with a fool; others may not be able to tell the difference.

Transition to the film clip by saying something like this:

A lot of people look for guidance in life, but seeking it in the wrong place is likely to do nothing but create problems. Let's take a look

at this satire about a guy who seeks wisdom in a place that's similar to what we've been looking at already.

Show the *Horror Scopes* film clip.

Bible Study

Idea #1: Ask your students to break into groups of four to six and assign each group all or a portion of the following passages to read: Exodus 15:13; Psalm 23; Psalm 25:5,9; Psalm 31:3; Psalm 32:8-10; and Isaiah 48:17. After they're finished reading, ask them to create a motto, bumper sticker, commercial jingle, or some other short summation of what these passages say about where we get our guidance.

You may want to get some discussion going by asking or assigning these next questions to your groups:

Why do you think people run to all kinds of odd—even nutty—people and things for guidance in life but ignore God?

Do you think most people really want guidance, or do they merely want a confirmation of their own wills and desires?

What are the primary ways God guides us?

What is the scary thing about allowing God to guide us? What is the comforting thing about allowing God to guide us?

How deep in the nitty-gritty things of life do you think God's guidance goes? To the people we should date or marry? To the kind of car we drive? To how we spend our money? To the kind of toothpaste we buy?

Is God's guidance usually specific in nature, or is it merely general principles to live by? Which is more demanding for us humans?

Idea #2: Ask your students to read the following passages: Exodus 15:13; Psalm 23; Psalm 25:5,9; Psalm 31:3; Psalm 32:8; and Isaiah 48:17. Then, working individually or in pairs, ask them to come up with a call and response set that spells out what the Bible says about guidance for human beings. A sample call and response might be—

> **Leader: When we are lost...**
> *People: He guides us!*

When your students finish, ask them to share their call and response with the group.

Engage your students with questions similar to those presented in Idea #1.

Wrap Up

Idea #1: Pass out blank pieces of paper to your students and ask them to finish the following statement: *For my life to genuinely be guided by God, I will need to_____.* Their answers should reflect what they are willing to do in order to allow God to guide them through this life. Ask only willing students to share what they have written. Close in prayer.

Idea #2: Many times God can't guide us because we are either too busy following something else, preoccupied, or filling our time and minds with way too many things that drown out His voice. Challenge your students to spend at least five minutes each day listening to God and reading His Word. Invite kids to make a commitment to go for it and ask someone to check with them next week to see if they fulfilled their five-minute listening commitment.

Production Notes: Mini Scrolls

Producer/Director Ryan Pettey

Mini Scrolls—who hasn't wondered about them? Who hasn't almost bought one? They hail as the kings of the impulse buy—the mini scroll. It started as just a simple question, and with the help of one too many Christopher Guest movies, became a reality.

Just who buys the mini scrolls anyway? *Horror Scopes*, originally an eight-minute movie, was re-shot and edited down into a more "service friendly" vignette. In February 2002, *Horror Scopes* was shot in two days with a loose script consisting mainly of scenes. Almost all the scenes were improvised, making for a very fun shoot with lots of outtakes. If anything, *Horror Scopes* finally sheds light on this often-overlooked relic of our society.

Part of the humor resides in the ridiculous idea that people might actually base their lives on a mini scroll, but when you think of the motivations many of us have for the lives we live, the mini scroll can seem like a comparatively wise option.

Adjustment 4

Alternate Routes

 ### Announcement Opener

Use just the last minute of the film clip and add your own announcement starting with "Don't get caught with your pants down...".

E-Message

Edit and download the latter part of this clip and send it to your students with a note encouraging them to "pay attention to the small details" (such as getting into God's Word, coming to youth group, and so on) so they don't trip and fall in their spiritual lives.

 ## Small Group

Focus: We need to be watchful of the small things that can trip us up.

Biblical basis: Matthew 25:1-13

Stuff you need: *Adjustment* video, Bibles, discussion questions

Getting Started

Adjustment is a silly film clip you can use to get a discussion rolling. Prepare your questions in advance keeping in mind the age level and maturity of your group as you create them. Open your session by showing—without much comment—the film clip. Introduce it by saying something like this: Take a look at this short film and see if you can come up with a theme for the video.

▶ *Adjustment* Film Clip

Show the film clip and get your students talking about a time when they missed an important detail—closing a door, turning off the faucet or stove, and so on.

Transition to the Bible study by asking a question like this—

This film clip is designed to prod us to think about the small details of life, which, if left undone, can really create problems for us. Let's take a look at a biblical warning regarding that idea.

 ## Bible Study

Ask your group to read Matthew 25:1-13, but before they start, give them some of the following background material for this passage so they'll better understand the wedding custom that's referred to by Jesus.

The exact role of the girls in the parable is uncertain. They could be part of the actual wedding party or merely servants whose chance to get to go to a massive, star-studded party comes when the Bridegroom (and probably his bride) shows up.

The lamps were most likely torches—rags soaked in oil to be used as part of a spectacular torchlight procession. A torch would typically burn for 15-20 minutes, but one that had been allowed to dry out would go out as soon as it was lit. (The suggested visual is of 10 desperate girls going through books of matches as they try to light a hopelessly dry torch, and then they all run out to the wedding parade.)

If you missed the processional, the gates were shut and you were banned from the party. Or if you happened to be *hired* to provide light, you would be fired for having no fire!

Now discuss the particulars in this story. Ask—

What small detail was overlooked?

What did it cost them?

Why was it overlooked?

How did they try to remedy their situation? What was the result?

What do you think about their excuse?

If the girls were employed to throw light for the wedding party, what would have been the just results?

Jesus said this parable is like a picture of God's kingdom. How do you think it reflects that kingdom?

What does the parable mean?

Move towards application to everyday life by asking questions such as—

* What are some small but important details that, if overlooked, will cause problems in our spiritual lives?

* What kinds of excuses do we often give ourselves for avoiding or not sweating those details?

* What message do you think this parable has for those of us who want to walk with God?

Wrap Up

Ask your group to think of one little—but important or necessary—detail they have let "dry out." This might be a spiritual discipline or a habit they once did but now seldom do, such as praying for a friend, writing thank you notes, or hugging their parents. Invite them to share that detail with another student and ask their friend to pray that

God will remind them to take care of that particular
detail during the week ahead.

Getting Started

The Detail Game

 Middle School

Focus: Putting God first is the missing detail in many lives.

Biblical basis: Luke 12:15-21

Stuff you need: a picture with lots of details, a prize, *Adjustment*
video, paper, pencils or pens, butcher paper, markers
or crayons, slips of paper

Find a busy picture with lots of detail. Study it and
jot down all the details you can see. Have pencils,
paper, and some kind of prize ready for your kids.
Make a copy of the picture on an overhead,
enlarge it, or post it in some way so that everyone
in the group can see it.

Tell your students: Sitting in your seats, I want you
to study this picture for 30 seconds and then I am
going to hide it. You will be given pencils and
paper and asked to list all of the things you
noticed about the picture. The one with the most
correct items wins a prize. Ready, set, go!!

After 30 seconds are up, turn the picture over
and give your kids a few minutes to record the
details they can remember. Go over the list and
give a prize to the kid with the longest and most
correct list.

▶ *Adjustment* Film Clip

Show your kids the *Adjustment* film clip. Ask questions such as—

> What do you think the filmmakers were saying with this short comedy?

> What was the one detail that caused all the problems?

Transition to the Bible study by saying something like this:

> **Let's take a look at a place in the Bible where an essential thing was overlooked and it made a big difference.**

 ## Bible Study

Divide your kids into groups of three to five students. Give each group one of the following assignments:

1. Read Luke 12:15-21 and write a diary or journal entry, as written by the main character in this parable, that reflects not only what he was busy doing and thinking about, but also the one important detail he left out of his life.

2. Read Luke 12:15-21 and create an exchange of letters between the main character in this story and his godly mother showing his frame of mind and her probable advice to him.

3. Read Luke 12:15-21 and create a short play about a pack of demons coming up with a plot to make sure the main character in the story gets everything he wants but not the main thing he needs.

4. Read Luke 12:15-21 and write a short jingle or dumb song that gives the main message about focusing in on the most important detail that was missed by the central character in the parable.

5. Read Luke 12:15-21 and retell this parable using a modern setting. Point out the missing vital detail in this person's life.

6. Read Luke 12:15-21 and create a mural or picture story that tells the tale of this man and his missing essential detail that cost him everything.

Now share and discuss the missing detail: Putting God First! Ask questions such as—

What tends to compete with God for our attention?

What should this rich guy have done to make him rich towards God?

Wrap Up

Pass out small slips of paper and pencils. Ask your students to imagine their lives broken down into dollars and cents. If $100 was a life that put God first in everything—a life rich towards God—and zero was a life without God, how *rich* do they think they are towards God? Invite your students to write a figure (not to be shared) on the slip of paper.

Close in prayer by saying something like this:

If you think you need more spiritual wealth in your life, add to your account today by inviting God to take first place in every area of your life.

High School

Focus: We need to keep an eye on the small but important spiritual details in our lives.

Biblical basis: Matthew 25:1-13

Stuff you need: a piece of poster board or a chalkboard, something to write with, *Adjustment* video, Adjustment Talksheet, 3x5 cards, video gear, paper, pencils or pens *(Note: You can download the* talksheet *from* www.YouthSpecialties.com/store/downloads code word: highway 2 *and photocopy it to use with your group.)*

FOR WANT OF A NAIL, THE SHOE WAS LOST,
FOR WANT OF THE SHOE, THE HORSE WAS LOST,
FOR WANT OF THE HORSE, THE RIDER WAS LOST,
FOR WANT OF THE RIDER, THE BATTLE WAS LOST,
FOR WANT OF THE BATTLE, THE KINGDOM WAS LOST,
AND ALL FOR THE WANT OF A HORSESHOE NAIL!

Getting Started

Write this old saying on a piece of poster board or a chalkboard and ask your students to explain its significance.

Transition to the film clip by saying something like this:

Let's take a look at a similar idea presented in a completely different fashion.

▶ *Adjustment* Film Clip

Before showing the film clip, get your students talking about a time when they missed an important detail and it caused them trouble—closing a door, turning off a faucet or the stove, and so on. Tell your students you have one more example of a missed detail and then show the *Adjustment* film clip.

Discuss the main concept of the film—one missing

detail and you end up on your face!

Move to the Bible study part of the session by saying something like this: This film clip is designed to prod us to think about the small details of our life, which, when left undone, can create some real problems for us. Let's take a look at one of Jesus' parables where keeping an eye on the details was everything!

Bible Study

Idea #1: Working individually, ask your students to complete The Tale of the Sputtering Torch talk-sheet. Before they start, give them some of the following background material for this passage so they'll better understand the wedding custom that's referred to by Jesus.

> The exact role of the girls in the parable is uncertain. They could be part of the actual wedding party or merely servants whose chance to get to go to a massive, star-studded party comes when the Bridegroom (and probably his bride) shows up.

> The lamps were most likely torches—rags soaked in oil to be used as part of a spectacular torchlight procession. A torch would typically burn for 15-20 minutes, but one that had been allowed to dry out would go out as soon as it was lit. (The suggested visual is of 10 desperate girls going through books of matches as they try to light a hopelessly dry torch, and then they all run out to the wedding parade.)

> If you missed the processional, the gates were shut and you were banned from the party. Or if you happened to be *hired* to provide light, you would be fired for having no fire!

The Tale of the Sputtering Torch

Read Matthew 25:1-13 and then write a letter that might be from one of the young women explaining, and perhaps trying to justify, why they were fired by the wedding planner and banished from parties at the King's house.

Ask your students to read their letters and discuss what *meaning* they can draw for everyday life. Discuss the "little details" that help us grow as Christians and talk about how we often depend on others to "light us up" when it's actually *our* job to fuel our own souls.

Idea #2: Using the parable of Matthew 25:1-13 as a base (make sure to grab the background material from Idea #1 and share that with your students before they read the passage), create an updated version of this story where a small detail causes someone to lose out on an important opportunity.

You may want to do this in a variety of ways:

Break into groups and create a skit or script for a new story.

Assign different stages of the story to each group to be acted out in front of everyone. When one group finishes their part, the next group should step up and share their part of the story, and so on until the parable is complete.

Make a short video of your interpretation. You can edit it during the week and show it to the whole group at the next meeting.

Make a rock opera of this story—bust out the drums and guitars and tell the story in a new way.

Film a trailer that could be shown in movie theaters. It should map out the essentials of the story about a missing detail and a massive disaster.

Create book titles that might tell the story in phases. You can make 'em silly if you want, like: *My Golden Wedding* by Annie Versary, *The Insurmountable Problem* by Major Setback, or *Don't Leave Without Me* by Isa Coming.

Have your kids share their creations and then zero in on what we need to be concerned with when it comes to details. Ask—

> What are some small but important details that, if overlooked, will cause problems in our spiritual lives?

> What kind of excuses do we often give ourselves for avoiding or not sweating those details?

> What message do you think this parable has for those of us who want to walk with God?

Wrap Up

Idea # 1: Ask your students to help you list some small—but essential—details that are necessary if we want to keep from drying out spiritually. Invite your group to spend some quiet time as they do some soul searching about any of these listed details that they may have been too busy to attend to lately. Ask a worship leader to close with a song that speaks of refreshing or renewing our souls.

Idea #2: Ask the students to come up with one detail they think they could commit to doing during the coming week that would help refuel their spiritual lives. Ask your kids to write the detail and their name and phone number on a 3x5 card and toss it into a container. Stir up the cards and redistribute them as you ask your students to add one more detail to their week—to call the person whose name is written on the card they've just received and give them a word of encouragement or hold them accountable by asking them if they've taken care of their spiritual detail yet.

Production Notes

Producer/Cinematographer Joe Perez

Like any normal day at Highway, Travis came up to me and told me to take the camera and the intern (Randy at the time since I still didn't know his name was Ryan) downtown, which was right around the corner, and film him stumbling down the street with his pants at his ankles. Travis: "Don't show the bottom half of his body until the end of the street when he stops and stands there realizing that he has his pants around his ankles... Get it??" I thought: Funny, this guy's going to get us arrested.

We arrive on the corner, and I'm thinking by this time in my career at Highway I'm already familiar with these types of shenanigans and still was unsure of the stunt we were about to pull. I said, "Okay Randy, you ready?"

There was an old couple sitting in front of us, probably wondering what these two young men were doing. One with camera in hand as the other performed the pee-pee dance out of nervousness. The time came, Ryan pulled down his pants, and started to stumble down the street--all while I was filming him and the others in the background being shocked out of their somnambulant states. Reaching the end of the street, I pulled away for the final frame, hit the camera's Stop button, and then we ran back to the office. One take, Jake baby!

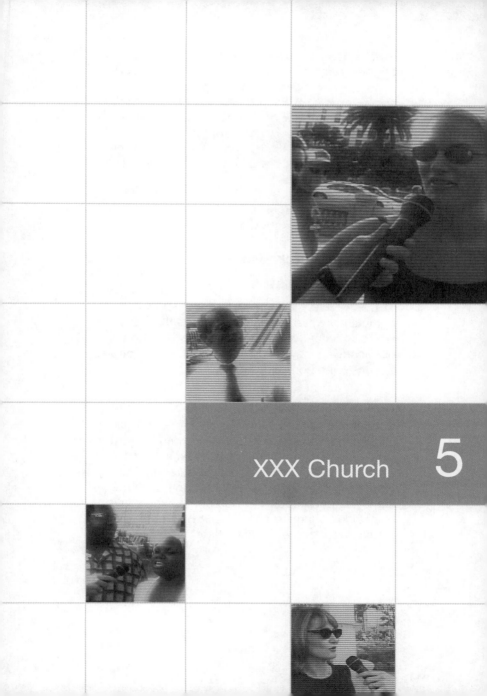

XXX Church 5

Note: Due to the subject matter of this video clip, the best results for an honest, influential lesson might be in smaller, single-sex groups with a same-sex leader. The lessons that follow are divided accordingly. It is also suggested that before using this lesson you take a tour of the xxxchurch.com Web site and familiarize yourself with what they are doing and how they can serve your students.

Alternate Routes

 ## General Church Use or
Emergent Ministries Use

This is a great clip to show to any audience, but particularly when sharing a message that deals with our culture or purity issues. We aren't doing our flocks any favors by assuming that few people struggle with pornography.

E-Mail Messages

Send a message to every kid on your e-mail list inviting them to check out www.xxxchurch.com. Don't tell them anything about it and see what kind of response you get. (Be prepared for the responses of some parents who don't quite understand the purpose of the Web site or why you'd want little Johnny to check it out because he would *never* look at a naked lady.)

Small Group
(For guys and a guy leader only.)

Focus: Dealing with sexual temptation.

Biblical basis: Matthew 5:28; 1 Corinthians 6:18-20; Hebrews 13:4; 2 Peter 2:18

Stuff you need: *XXXChurch* video, Bibles, discussion questions

Getting Started

Sit your guys down and show the *XXXChurch* film clip. Ask your guys questions such as—

> Do you think porn affects guys in a negative way? Why or why not?
>
> Do you think most girls are as interested in porn as guys are? Why or why not?
>
> Do you think becoming a Christian makes your interest in naked girls go away? Why or why not?
>
> What's the difference between hard and soft porn?
>
> Is it okay for a Christian guy to check out the soft stuff?
>
> Do you often get porn ads coming through your e-mail? Have you ever clicked on a site and been surprised by porn? *(Porn companies have purchased some Christian-sounding domains.)*
>
> Is it easy to delete those things, or is it tempting to take a closer look?

Transition to the Bible study part of the lesson by saying something like this:

Most guys know there is something seedy or wrong about checking out porn, but a lot of guys don't really know why. Let's take a few minutes to read and discuss what the Bible says and what we can do about it.

Bible Study

Read this passage from *The Message* to your guys: "But don't think you've preserved your virtue simply by staying out of bed. Your heart can be corrupted by lust even quicker than your body. Those leering looks you think nobody notices—they also corrupt." (Matthew 5:28) Ask—

What is Jesus saying here?

What does lust corrupt? How does it corrupt?

If a woman is simply an "object" in the mind of a guy, is that corrupting to his soul? How?

Do you think a married guy who gets hot thinking about his wife or seeing her nude is lusting? If so, is it wrong? If no, what's the difference?

Now read this passage in which Peter is talking about those who would yank down a believer: "For they mouth empty, boastful words and, by appealing to the lustful desires of sinful human nature, they entice people who are just escaping from those who live in error." (2 Peter 2:18, NIV)

Ask—

Do those in the sex business simply want to use their freedom of expression to provide an educational Web site, or do you think they're trying to create an addiction in the men who surf those kinds of sites? If the latter, what devices do they use to draw guys into this trap?

Can looking at porn become addictive? Why or why not?

Do you think most Christian guys pretend they are not attracted by sexual images? If you think yes, why do they try to hide what is obvious to everyone else?

Do you think exposure to images can "pervert" a guy? Why or why not?

Read the following passage from The Message:

"There is a sense in which sexual sins are different from all others. In sexual sin we violate the sacredness of our own bodies, these bodies that were made for God-given and God-modeled love, for 'becoming one' with another. Or didn't you realize that your body is a sacred place, the place of the Holy Spirit? Don't you see that you can't live however you please, squandering what God paid such a high price for? The physical part of you is not some piece of property belonging to the spiritual part of you. God owns the whole works. So let people see God in and through your body." (1 Corinthians 6:18-20)

Ask—

If you had a wife (or even a girlfriend), do you think she would be fine with you checking out *Playboy* or logging on to a naked lady Web site? Why or why not?

Does hitting porn sites or checking out mags make it harder or easier to control sexual urges? Why?

Now read this passage from *The Message*:

"Honor marriage, and guard the sacredness of sexual intimacy between wife and husband. God draws a firm line against casual and illicit sex." (Hebrews 13:4)

Ask—

How does porn mess up the sacredness of sexual intimacy between a wife and husband?

Does porn fit the category of casual and illicit sex? Why or why not?

Wrap Up

Encourage your students to get online and sign up for the accountability program offered by xxxchurch.com. This is a free download that will

enable a computer to send any Web sites a person
visits to two accountability partners.
Close in prayer.

Getting Started

Show your girls the *XXXChurch* film clip. Get into
small groups for discussion. Make sure to have a

Small Group
(For girls and a female leader only.)

Focus: *God calls all women to sexual purity and appropriate-
ness.*

Biblical basis: *Matthew 19:4-6; 1 Corinthians 6:18-20; 1 Timothy 2:9*

Stuff you need: XXXChurch *video, Bibles, discussion questions, talksheets (Note: You can download the Talksheet from*
www.YouthSpecialties.com/store/downloads *code word:*
highway 2 *and photocopy it to use with your group.)*

female leader in each group.

Get the discussion going by asking your girls
questions such as—

Do you think girls have as much of a problem with
pornography as guys do? Why or why not?

What do you think of women who allow themselves to be used in porn sites?

Why do you think they do this?

If you were offered a lot of money to pose nude,
would you be tempted to do it?

What kinds of problems does it create for girls if
they are desired for what they have or what they
are willing to do with a guy rather than for who
they are?

Transition to the Bible study by saying something like this:

> **Many guys struggle with sexual self-control. Because God created guys to be easily aroused by visual images, stuff like porn feeds right into their psyches. At the same time, girls often seem clueless about the fact that how they dress affects guys' sexual self-control. And while it's true that an attractive woman will get the interest of a guy regardless of how she is dressed, a Christian girl who dresses like a "ho" (hooker) is sending all the wrong messages.**

> **The Bible doesn't tell girls what to wear, but it gives some great operating principles on all facets of our sexual behavior and how we "advertise" ourselves. Let's start by reviewing God's design for sexual behavior.**

 ## *Bible Study*

Ask your girls to explain the meaning of this old proverb in terms of sexuality:

> *"Why buy the cow if you can get the milk for free?"* (Note that a lot of girls and women give away their sexuality cheap or in exchange for a potential relationship—and many of them end up feeling used in the process.)

Invite your students to check out God's design for sexuality from the pages of His Word. In groups of three to four ask your girls to read the following passages and have them answer the questions relating to each verse:

> Matthew 19:4-6 — What is God's purpose for sexuality?

> 1 Corinthians 6:18-20 — What is the problem with sexual relationships outside of the committed context of marriage?

What would this passage say about women who allow themselves to be used sexually?

What should a guy be required to do before being allowed the privilege of a sexual relationship with a girl?

Who usually loses when those requirements are set aside? Why?

Transition to the next part of the Bible study by saying something like this:

We can see what God wants for us sexually and romantically—and most girls would prefer His design for their lives! But often we send guys a different signal by being careless or inappropriate in our choice of clothes or behavior.

Share this verse with your girls:

What is a "sensible" manner of dressing?

Describe what kind of clothing is appropriate for a Christian girl and what kind isn't.

Do you think most girls dress in order to attract guys?

"And the women should be the same way, quiet and sensible in manner and clothing."

(1 Timothy 2:9), The Living Bible

Do you think girls who dress in a revealing way know it makes guys think about them sexually?

Why is it unwise to advertise yourself as a sex object?

How would you go about telling a friend she dresses like a "ho"?

How is it showing love for our brothers if we are intentional and sensible about how we dress?

Wrap Up

This is the NOHO pledge from the xxxchurch.com Web site. We've printed it on our talksheet with their permission. You can download and make a

copy of it for your girls to read, discuss, and perhaps modify—especially if dress styles change and
some new sordid fashion becomes all the rage.

Take The NoHo Pledge

I, _____, promise to the best of my
ability not to dress, buy clothes or act like a Ho.
Clothes I should try to avoid buying or wearing:
tight pants that are cut so low that when I bend
over you can see my g-string or butt crack, tight
half shirts that show my six or not-so-six pack,
tight shirts that are low cut to show my cleavage
or short shorts that you can see my butt cheeks in.

I know that God desires me to glorify him in all
things and I realize that by dressing like a Ho, I
only desire to give glory to me, not God. I also
know boys have a problem with sexual things and
I know that by not dressing like a Ho, I can be a
part of the solution, not the problem!

And now here's one for guys to sign. Read it, talk
about, pray, and then sign. And live it.

Take the PorNO Pledge

I, _____, promise to the be accountable to someone, whether it is a friend, a relative, or a pastor. I realize if I try and do this on my own, I'm going to jack it up. I will be open and real about my own struggles and talk about the dirty little secret and encourage others to be real and open about it. I will put safeguards in my life to keep my away from the crud. If it means I've got to get rid of the satellite dish and DSL, then I will do it.

I am not ashamed to be human and realize that mama was right...honesty is the best policy.

After a time of prayer and discussion, offer the girls an opportunity to sign their copy of the pledge.

XXXChurch Production Notes

Producer Javad Shadzi

The church, for the most part, is good about

addressing issues that plague believers of Christ, but one topic has been somewhat neglected—pornography use. Because of this, when www.xxxchurch.com approached us and asked if we'd be interested in teaming up with them to do a video about society's perceptions of pornography, we were more than happy to oblige. www.xxxchurch.com is a new organization that has begun to address the issue of pornography use among Christians. Their Web site is chock-full of stats and resources that help call pornography use to light and address it.

For this video clip, the guys for xxxchurch.com headed to Las Vegas to hit the streets and find out what the average person really thinks about pornography. We were quite surprised by some of the responses, but for the most part people have become desensitized to pornography. It has gone from being something derogatory and disrespectful that you hide to being basically just a choice you can make. People seem to have forgotten that pornography is more than just a "choice", it can shape your perception of how you see the opposite sex, it can take a friend and make them the object of lust, and it leads to more and more lustful thoughts. It really made us consider the effects of sexually explicit material in our own lives. Even if it's just a picture in a catalog or a steamy movie love scene—all pornography leads us away from the sexual reality God has intended for our lives.